Copyright 2017 by Elise Sanders All rights reserved.

In no way is it legal to reproduce, duplicate, or transmit any part of this document in either electronic means or in printed format. Recording of this publication is strictly prohibited and any storage of this document is not allowed unless with written permission from the publisher. All rights reserved.

The information provided herein is stated to be truthful and consistent, in that any liability, in terms of inattention or otherwise, by any usage or abuse of any policies, processes, or directions contained within is the solitary and utter responsibility of the recipient reader. Under no circumstances will any legal responsibility or blame be held against the publisher for any reparation, damages, or monetary loss due to the information herein, either directly or indirectly.

Respective authors own all copyrights not held by the publisher.

The information herein is offered for informational purposes solely, and is universal as so. The presentation of the information is without contract or any type of guarantee assurance.

The trademarks that are used are without any consent, and the publication of the trademark is without permission or backing by the trademark owner. All trademarks and brands within this book are for clarifying purposes only and are the owned by the owners themselves, not affiliated with this document.

INSTANT POT COOKBOOK

The Ultimate Healthy Delicious Recipes Cookbook

Elise Sanders

Contents

INSTANT POT COOKBOOK 2

The Ultimate Healthy Delicious Recipes Cookbook 2

Introduction 3

Chapter 1 : Most Healthiest Spices 11

Chapter 2 : Seafood Recipes 14

Chapter 3: Chicken Recipes 24

Chapter 4: Pork Recipes 38

Chapter 5 Beef Recipes 53

Chapter 6 Turkey Recipes 67

Chapter 7 Lamb Recipes 77

Conclusion 85

Introduction

I want to thank you and congratulate you for downloading the book, *"Instant Pot Cookbook, The Ultimate Healthy Delicious Recipes Cookbook".*

I hope that after purchasing this book, you will be amazed by how easy and convenient it is to have an instant pot in your kitchen and how quick and nutritious your family's meals can be. Thanks again for downloading this book, I hope you enjoy it!

⁕ SO Why Instant Pot?

Instant pot is an energy saving method, which can save up to an enormous 70% of your power bill. Wouldn't it be nice to reduce energy and your consumption of electricity in order to decrease the amount of money that you pay each month in bills? YES!!!

Very convenient: there are one-touch keys for most of the cooking tasks and multiple usages for all your healthy and nutritious meals. Instant pot preserves more nutrients in your food as it takes less time to cook, then that also means more vitamins and nutrients will not be eliminated from your food.

Manufacture specifications:

With your Instant Pot, you can tailor for various cooking results and recipes. Instant Pot is programmed with adjustable cooking modes, up to 24 hours of delayed cooking, and automatic keep warm for up to 10 hours. Most traditional, modern and international recipes can easily be adapted for Instant Pot.

Instant Pot's elegant and durable industrial design makes it easy to clean and pleasurable to use. The stainless steel inner pot and lid are both dishwasher safe while the cooker base can easily be wiped clean with a damp cloth.

Instant Pot is carefully designed with all models passing stringent UL and ULC certifications, giving users uncompromised safety and peace of mind. Instant Pot protects users with the following 10 proven safety mechanisms:

- ❖ Safety Lid Lock prevents accidental opening while cooker is pressurized.
- ❖ Pressure Regulator ensures working pressure is under the safety limit of 15.23 psi.
- ❖ Leaky Lid Smart Detection (eg. steam release is at open position).
- ❖ Anti-Blockage Vent prevents food debris from blocking the vent.
- ❖ Magnetic Sensor for Lid Position Detection monitors whether the lid is in an unsafe zone for pressure cooking.
- ❖ Automatic Pressure Control keeps pressure in a safe range.
- ❖ Excess Pressure Protection releases excess pressure into internal chamber in the event of a dangerous situation.
- ❖ Automatic Temperature Control regulates temperatures based on the type of program selected.
- ❖ High Temperature Monitoring prevents food from burning.
- ❖ Fuse Cuts Off Power when electrical current or temperature exceeds safety limits.

Instant Pot

Instant Pot

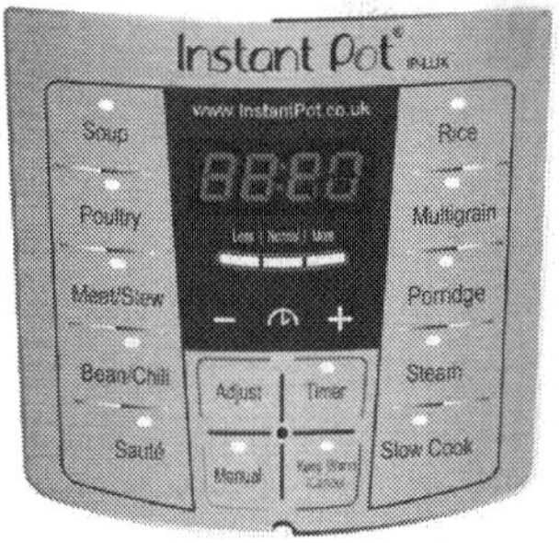
Instant Pot
www.InstantPot.co.uk
Soup
Rice
Poultry
Multigrain
Meat/Stew
Porridge
Bean/Chili
Steam
Sauté
Slow Cook
Less | Normal | More
Adjust
Timer
Manual

Instant Pot
www.InstantPot.com
Soup
Rice
Poultry
Multigrain
Meat/Stew
Congee
Bean/Chili
Steam
Adjust
Timer
Sauté
Slow Cook
Manual

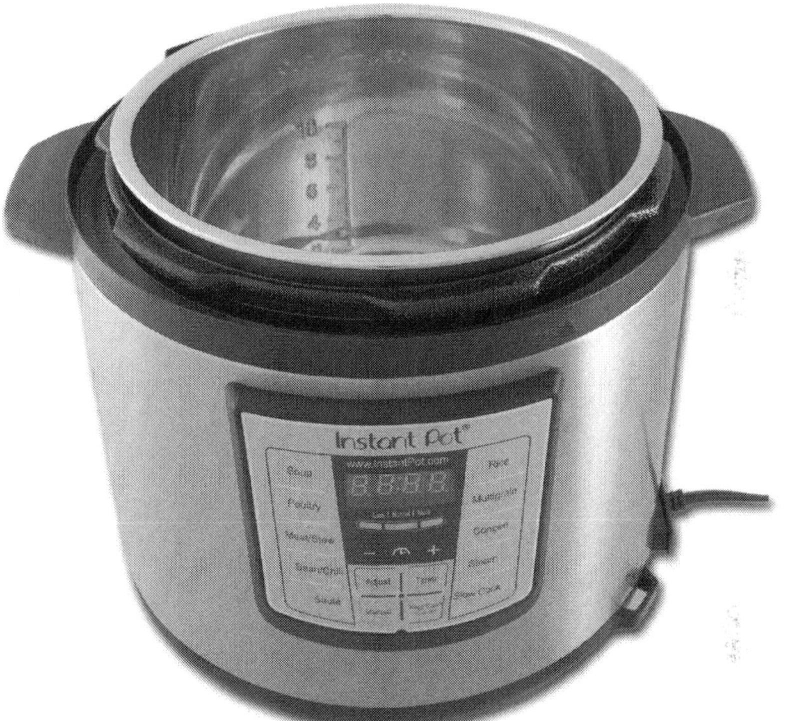
Instant Pot
Soup
Poultry
Rice

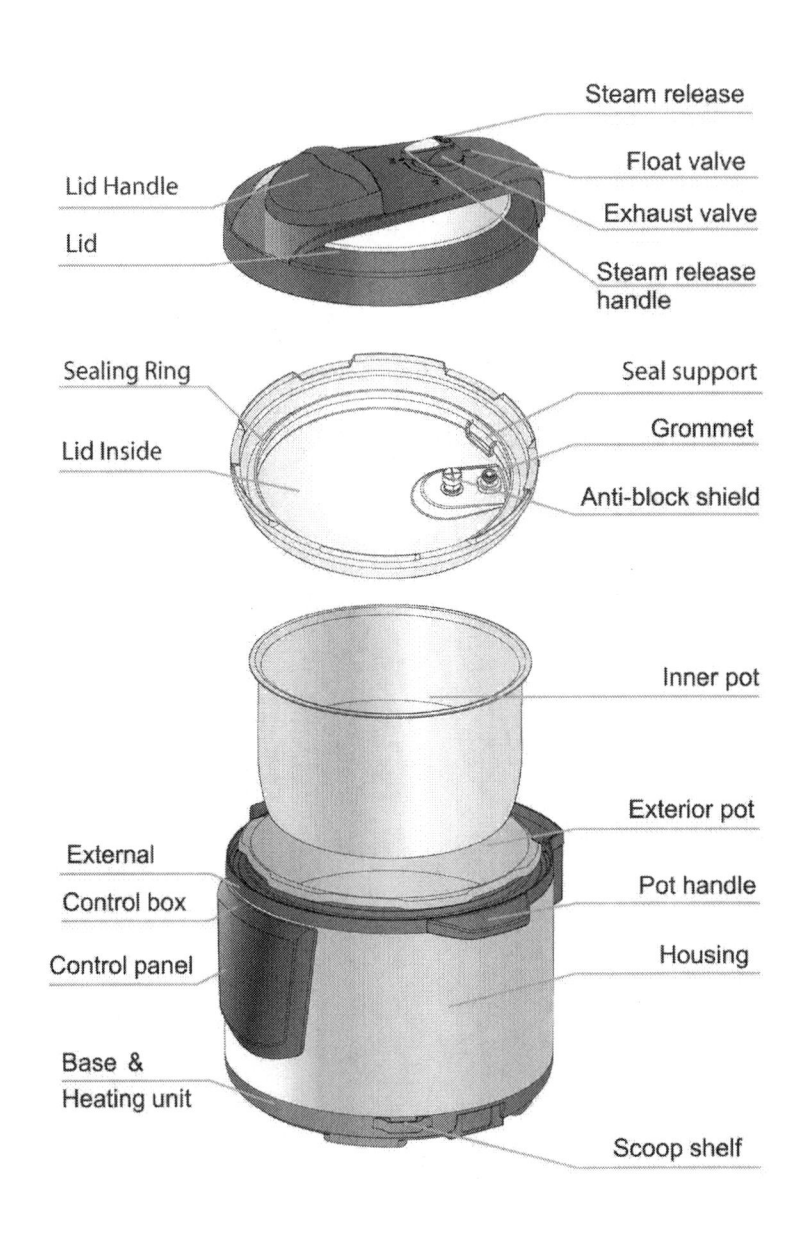

- Lid Handle
- Lid
- Steam release
- Float valve
- Exhaust valve
- Steam release handle
- Sealing Ring
- Lid Inside
- Seal support
- Grommet
- Anti-block shield
- Inner pot
- Exterior pot
- External Control box
- Control panel
- Base & Heating unit
- Pot handle
- Housing
- Scoop shelf

Chapter 1 : Most Healthiest Spices

1) **Turmeric** : Turmeric provides anti-inflammatory properties, which is why it can be helpful with a long list of conditions and disorders brought about by excessive inflammation. Turmeric can be used as an all-natural way to treat the symptoms of arthritis, and to sooth the digestive system.

2) **Rosemary:** Rosemary contains substances that are useful for stimulating the immune system, increasing circulation, and improving digestion. Rosemary also contains anti-inflammatory compounds that may make it useful for reducing the severity of asthma attacks. In addition, rosemary has been shown to increase the blood flow to the head and brain, improving concentration

3) **Basil:** Here are the benefits of Basil- Anti-inflammatory, antioxidant, cancer-fighter,fever-reducer,diabetes-preventer,liver-protector,blood vessel-protector, anti-stress solution,immune-booster

4) **Nutmeg:** Nutmeg has detoxifying properties, which is why it is used as an ingredient in many detox beverages and cleansing programs. It can spur the liver to expel toxins and helps expunge the kidneys of impurities.

5) **Saffron**: it has been shown to be an effective treatment for depression, as well as menstrual cramping.

6) **Curry**: Curry is known to be cancer prevention, pain relief and inflamation, protect the heart, protects bones, antibacterial, liver detox, etc

7) **Thyme:** It lower blood pressure, stop the coughing, boost your immunity, disinfect, boots your moods

8) **Ginger:** Digestive tract protection, brain health, help calm nausea, migraine relief, protect from UV rays, stable blood sugar lavel, promote health, help muscle aches , weight lost.

9) **Cinnamon**: Lower your cholesterol, help treat diabetes, anti- fungal, reduce risk of parkinson diseas, anti -inflammatory properties

10) **Parsley:** It has Vitamin K, excellent source of beta carotene, support healthy kidneys, anti-inflammatory properties, relief pains, provide daily iron, anti- cancer cell

Chapter 2 : Seafood Recipes

Shrimp with Rice

Ingredients

- 1 jalapeno chopped pepper
- 2 cups finely chopped tomatoes
- 1 tablespoon olive oil
- 1½ pounds peeled and deveined shrimp
- ¼ teaspoon crushed red pepper flakes
- Pinch of salt
- 1 cup chicken broth
- ¼ cup chopped scallion
- 1 large red bell pepper
- 2 chopped celery stalks
- 2 minced garlic cloves
- 1 cup long grain white rice

1. **Instructions:** Pour the oil in the Instant Pot and select "Sauté." Then add the shrimp and sprinkle with half the red pepper flakes, a pinch of salt and black pepper. Cook for about 4 minutes. Transfer the shrimp into a bowl. Then add onion, bell pepper and celery, and cook for about 5 minutes. Add garlic, jalapeño, remaining red pepper flakes and black pepper, and sauté for about 1 minute.

Select "Cancel" and stir in the tomatoes, rice and broth, then mix thoroughly

"High Pressure" for about 7 minutes. Select the "Cancel" button and carefully do a quick release.

Remove the lid and immediately stir in the cooked shrimp. Secure the lid right away and keep aside for about 5 minutes before serving.

Fish Chowder

Ingredients

- 1 cup of fish stock
- 1 finely chopped rib of celery
- 1 tablespoon of light butter
- 1 finely chopped carrot
- A pinch of dried thyme
- ½ cup of corn kernels
- ½ cup of full-fat milk
- ½ large, finely chopped onion
- ½ cup of chilled water
- 1 finely chopped potato
- ½ pound of any white fish fillets
- 1 small bay leaf

Instructions:

Put the butter in your cooker and set to Medium.
Fry the onions until they have softened.
Add the carrot, bay leaf. potatoes,the stock, fish, water, thyme and celery, and fry for about a minute.

Secure the lid and put on high pressure. Cook for 4 minutes, then take the bay leaf out. Add the corn and the milk and stir well, then season as required,then cook on medium heat until they all cook through. Serve with parsley and enjoy.

Curry Fish

Ingredients

- 1¼ cups chopped tomatoes
- 1 seeded and chopped Serrano pepper,
- 1 tablespoon fresh lemon juice
- 2 minced garlic cloves
- 2 tablespoons curry powder
- 2 teaspoons ground cumin
- 2 teaspoons ground coriander
- 1 tablespoon olive oil
- 2 curry leaves
- 2 medium chopped onions
- 1 tablespoon finely grated fresh ginger
- 1 teaspoon red chili powder
- ½ teaspoon ground turmeric
- 2 cups unsweetened coconut milk
- 1½ pound fish fillets, cut into bite size

Instructions:

Pour the oil in the Instant Pot and select "Sauté." Add the curry leaves and cook for about 30 seconds. Add ginger and garlic, onion and cook for about 5 minutes, add some spices, pour in the coconut milk stir. Select "Cancel" and put in fish, tomatoes and Serrano pepper.

Secure the lid and cook under "Manual" and "Low Pressure" for about 5 minutes, then Select the "Cancel"

Remove the lid and put in some lemon juce evenly, then Serve hot and enjoy.

❋ Mussels Dish

Ingredients:

- ❖ Freshly ground black pepper
- ❖ 2 pound of cleaned mussels,
- ❖ 1 tablespoon olive oil
- ❖ 1 medium chopped onion
- ❖ 1 cup low-sodium chicken broth
- ❖ 2 tablespoons fresh lemon juice
- ❖ 1 minced garlic clove
- ❖ ½ teaspoon crushed dried rosemary

Instructions:

Pour the oil in the Instant Pot and select "Sauté." Add the onion and cook for about 4 minutes. Add garlic and rosemary and sauté for about 1 minute.

Select "Cancel" and stir in the broth, lemon juice and black pepper.

Secure the lid and cook under "Manual" and "Low Pressure" for about 1 minute. Select the "Cancel" button and carefully do a quick release.

Remove the lid and transfer the mussels to the serving bowl and top with the sauce liquid from the pot. Serve while hot

✤ Salmon Dish

Ingredients:

- salt and pepper
- 4 salmon fillets
- 1 white shaved onion
- 4 sprigs of parsley
- 3 sliced tomatoes
- 1 lemon, sliced
- 4 sprigs of thyme
- olive oil

Instructions:

In this Order lay the ingredients on the parchment paper : a swirl of oil, a layer of potatoes, salt, pepper and oil, fish fillets, salt, pepper and oil, herbs, onion rings, lemon slices, salt, and oil.

Wrap the packet snugly in tinfoil.

Put 2 cups of water in the pressure cooker. Place the steamer basket in position and lay the packet on the steamer, put the fish, and close the cook top, turn on high heat to let it reach the pressure Then, turn down the heat to the lowest setting.

Cooking time should be between 11 to 14 minutes

then you can release the vapour but do NOT open the top just yet, wait for another 5 minutes. Then serve hot and enjoy.

⁕ Lobster Tails Butter Dish

Ingredients:

- 1 cup water
- 2 pound lobster tails, cut in half
- 2 tablespoons melted light butter
- Pinch of salt

Instructions:

Add 1 cup of the water in the Instant Pot. Arrange the lobster tails, shell side in the trivet.

Secure the lid and cook under "Manual" and "Low Pressure" for about 4 minutes, then select the "Cancel" button and carefully do a quick release.

Remove the lid and transfer the tails to the serving plate. Drizzle with butter and sprinkle with salt and serve.

⁕ Prawn Rice Dish

Ingredients:
- 1 1/2cups chicken broth
- 4 cloves of minced garlic
- 1/4 cup chopped fresh Parsley
- 1 teaspoon sea salt
- 1 pound medium shrimp
- 1cup Jasmine Rice
- 1/4 cup butter

- 1 medium lemon, juiced
- 1 pinch saffron
- 1/4 teaspoon black pepper
- 1 pinch crushed red pepper
- Optional- (chopped fresh Parsley, Lemon Juice, grated hard cheese parmesan)

Instrsuctions:

Combine all ingredients in your pressure cooker
Secure lid and cook under high pressure for 5 minutes.
Quickly released by turning the valve of an electric multi cooker or placing a stove top unit under cool running water

The paella can be served with the shells on the shrimp or, If desired, then remove cooked shrimp from the rice and peel. Put back the peeled shrimp into the rice and serve(discard the shells).
Serve fresh parsley, butter, grated cheese and a squeeze of lemon juice.

🞣 Yummy Cod Fish Dish

Ingredients:

- Pinch of salt
- Freshly ground black pepper
- 1 pound(halved) cherry tomatoes
- 4 ounce cod fillets
- 2 minced garlic cloves

- ❖ 2 tablespoons chopped fresh rosemary
- ❖ 1 tablespoon olive oil

Instructions:

Grease a large heat-proof bowl. Place half of the cherry tomatoes in the bottom of the prepared bowl, then followed by the rosemary. Prepare the bowl in the instant pot, then single layer the cod fillets, followed by the remaining tomatoes. Sprinkle with garlic and drizzle with oil.

Secure the lid and cook under "Manual" and "High Pressure" for about 5 minutes. Select the "Cancel" button and carefully do a quick release.

Remove the lid and transfer the fish fillets and tomatoes on serving plates. Sprinkle with salt and black pepper, and then serve.

Chapter 3: Chicken Recipes

Elise Sanders

Chicken Corn Dish

Ingredients:

- 1 cup cooked chopped bacon
- 1/2 cup Pepper Jack shredded cheese
- 2 teaspoons red chili powder
- 1 teaspoon ground cumin
- 14-ounce fresh corn kernel, softened
- 7 ounce cream cheese,
- 2 tablespoons olive oil
- 1 1/4 cups chopped onion
- 2 teaspoons minced garlic
- 2/3 cup jalapeño seeded and chopped peppers
- 1 teaspoon dried crushed oregano
- 31/2 cups cooked chopped chicken
- 2 cups finely chopped tomatoes
- 2½ cups low-sodium chicken broth

Instructions: Pour the oil in the Instant Pot and select "Sauté." Then add the onion and cook for about 4 minutes.

Select "Cancel" and stir in the remaining ingredients except cream cheese, bacon and Pepper Jack cheese.

Secure the lid and select "Soup" and just use the default time of 10 minutes. Select the "Cancel" button and carefully do a quick release.

Remove the lid and stir in the cream cheese and a ½ cup of the bacon. Select "Sauté" and cook for about 3 minutes. Top with the remaining bacon and Pepper Jack cheese and serve hot.

Chicken Coca Cola Dish

Ingredients:

- 4 chicken drumsticks
- Salt and pepper
- 1 tablespoon balsamic vinegar
- 1 small chopped chilli
- 1 large finely chopped onion
- 2 cups Coca Cola
- 2 tablespoon olive oil

Instructions: Heat the oil in the cooker, add chicken pieces and brown well.

Remove the chicken and brown onion in juices.

Add balsamic vinegar, chilli and Coca Cola.

Return chicken to pot, season to taste, close the pressure cooker and bring to pressure. Cook for 10 min.

Release the pressure and remove the lid.

Serve and enjoy!

♦ Roasted Chicken

Ingredients:

- 1 whole chicken, neck and giblets removed
- 2 tablespoons olive oil
- 1 tablespoon fresh minced rosemary
- ½ tablespoon crushed red pepper flakes
- Freshly ground black pepper
- ½ tablespoon ground cumin
- ½ tablespoon cayenne pepper

Instructions: Generously rub the chicken with the spice mixture rosemary and spices.

Pour the oil in the Instant Pot and select "Sauté." Add the chicken and cook for about 8 minutes or until browned

Select the "Cancel" button, then secure the lid and select "Poultry," using the default time of 20 minutes. Select the "Cancel" button and carefully do a quick release.

Remove the lid and flip the side of the chicken. Next, secure the lid and cook under "Manual" and "High Pressure" for about 15 minutes. Select the "Cancel" button and carefully do a quick release.

Remove the lid and transfer onto a platter. Keep aside for about 5-10 minutes before slicing.

Chicken Ginger Dish

Ingredients:
- ¼ cup soya sauce
- ¼ cup water
- 1 piece finely grated fresh ginger -
- ¼ cup dry sherry
- 1 chicken cut into pieces
- 1 large finely diced onion

Instructions:

Heat pressure cooker with some oil.(please make sure lid off)

Put the chicken in until brown, then sprinkle the chicken with the onion and ginger, mix well, then add sherry, soya sauce and water.

Close the lid, and when full pressure is reached reduce the heat and cook for 8 minutes , then add a pinch of salt and pepper. Serve and enjoy.

Honey Chicken Drumstick Dish

Ingredients:
- 2 pounds Chicken drumsticks

- ❖ 1 cup chicken stock
- ❖ 1 tablespoons olive oil
- ❖ 1 cup honey
- ❖ ½ cup soy sauce
- ❖ 1 medium diced Onion
- ❖ 2 cloves minced garlic
- ❖ ¼ teaspoon red pepper flakes
- ❖ ¼ teaspoons salt
- ❖ ¼ teaspoons black pepper

Instructions: In the mixing bowl, put the chicken drumsticks and marinates with 2 cloves minced garlic, ¼ teaspoons salt, ¼ teaspoons black pepper, ¼ teaspoon red pepper flakes, 1 cup of honey, and 1/2 cup soy sauce

In your pressure cooker sauté the diced onions with olive oil for about 3 minutes, then add the chicken stock. Bring to a boil, then add your marinated chicken drumsticks along with any sauce in the mixing bowl. Lock lid and cook on High for 30 minutes.

Release pressure naturally once timer goes off, and carefully remove the drumsticks to a serving platter. Serve with rice or pasta, and salad or herb of your choice

❧ Chicken Savory Dish

Ingredients:

- 4 chicken breasts
- 1 teaspoon dried parsley flakes
- 1 tablespoon of butter
- ½ cup water
- 2 cups chicken broth
- 1 teaspoon sea salt
- 1/2 pound of baby carrots
- 1 zucchini, sliced

Instructions:

Place chicken breasts in pressure cooker with the chicken broth, sea salt, dried parsley flakes and butter. Lock lid and cook on Low pressure for 20. Set timer. Once timer goes off, release pressure naturally. Open your lid and add in your baby carrots and sliced zucchini.

Once you have surrounded your chicken breasts with the baby carrots and sliced zucchini, add in the ½ cup of your water and lock lid. Cook on High for another 20 minutes.

Once timer goes off, release pressure naturally and check that everything is nice and soft. Serve with rice or noodles with fresh ground pepper.

♣ Chicken Noodles Soup

Ingredients:

- 4 Pounds of Chicken Breasts
- 5 Carrots
- 3 Ribs of Diced Celery
- 1 Cup of Peas
- Salt and Pepper
- 1 Sprig of Thyme
- 1 Teaspoon of Olive Oil
- 2 Onions
- 6 Cups of Chicken Broth
- 2 Cups of Egg Noodles
- 1 Teaspoon of unsalted Butter

Instructions:

Press the sauté button on the pressure cooker, then add oil to the cooker, stir fry the onions until soft, put carrots and celery and stir together for about 6 minutes

Season your chicken breasts with salt and pepper and then place in with the stir fry mixture, pour the chicken broth, thyme, then parsley, and shut the lid, cook for 8 minutes on high pressure

Once the eight minutes are up, perform a quick release of the pressure, then wait about 5 more minutes before removing the lid

Get rid of the herbs in the mixture and transfer the pieces of chicken to a cutting board .On the cutting board, shred the chicken meat , then place back in the pot, press the browning button, when boil, cancel the browning and press simmer button

Add in the noodles as the mixture begins to simmer, then wait for noodles to be cooked, add the peas, and mix evenly, shut of the cooker, then serve and enjoy.

Chicken Marsala

Ingredients:

- Cooked penne pasta
- 16 ounces of Chicken breats
- 2 cup sliced onion
- 2 sprig of fresh thyme
- 2.5 teaspoons salt
- 4 teaspoons minced garlic
- 6 tablespoons of all-purpose flour
- 1.5 teaspoon freshly grounded black pepper
- 7 tablespoons unsalted butter
- 4 teaspoons of fresh thyme leaves
- 22 ounces stemmed and sliced mushrooms

- ❖ 1.5 cup of Marsala
- ❖ 4 cups of homemade chicken stock

Instructions: Marinates the chicken with 2 teaspoons of salt and 1 tsp pepper. Heat 2 tablespoon butter in a pressure cooker.

Cook the chicken brown evenly, then put aside.

Put 6 tbsp butter into the pressure cooker and then put onions along with thyme sprig. Sauté those about 4 minutes.

Put the mushrooms and stir, add garlic, ½ teaspoons of salt, and 1/2 tsp pepper. Slowly add the flour and cook for 3 minutes. Stir in Marsala and then simmer about 5 minutes.

Now pour the chicken-stock and shift the chicken breasts back to the cooker. Cover the cooker and cook for 3 minutes under low pressure.

Prepare the pasta in boiling salted-water according to the Preparation give on the package.

Uncover the cooker after steam is released. put the chicken and dump thyme sprig. Simmer and let the sauce thicken. Add thyme leaves and serve "chicken marsala" over pasta.

⚜ Potatos Mashed Chicken Dish

Ingredients:

- ❖ 1 lb boneless skinless chicken breasts
- ❖ 2 Tablespoons kosher salt
- ❖ 1/2 Tablespoon white pepper
- ❖ 2 Cups of beef stock

- 1/4 cup butter
- 1/2 Cup milk
- 6 Cups cold water
- 3 Pounds peeled and sliced potatoes
- 500 Grams green peas.

Instructions: In a mixing bowl, add 3 cups of water and the beef stock. Place the chicken in the pressure cooker and pour the liquids. Press poultry and cook for 30 minutes.

Once time is up, allow the pressure to rescind. Transfer the chickens to a plate and shred, then sauté for 5 minutes, put aside

In a pressure cooker, bring 3 cups water to boil, add the potatoes and peas. Cook on high pressure for 30 minutes.

Allow the pressure to disappear naturally. Drain the potatoes and peas, return to the pressure cooker, then add milk and butter.

Mash the mixture and cover for 5 minutes, then season with the salt and white pepper, Garnish with coriander. Serve hot with chicken and enjoy .

Sour Garlic Chicken Dish

Ingredients:

- 2 pounds chicken breasts or thighs
- 1/4 teaspoon paprika
- 1/4 cup white cooking wine
- 5 minced garlic cloves

- 1 cup organic chicken broth
- 1 large lemon juiced
- 5 teaspoons arrowroot
- 1 teaspoon sea salt
- 1 diced onion
- 1 teaspoon dried parsley
- 1 tablespoon avocado oil

Instructions: Turn Instant Pot onto the saute feature and place in the diced onion and cooking oil, leave onions on for 8 minutes, or brown

Add in the remaining ingredients except for the arrowroot flour and secure the lid.

Select the "Poultry" and allow cook time to complete, release steam and carefully remove lid

Thicken the sauce by making a slurry. To do this remove about 1/4 cup sauce from the pot, add in the arrowroot flour, and then reintroduce the slurry into the remaining liquid. Stir and serve while hot.

Spicy Chicken Soup

Ingredients:

- 4 Chicken Breasts
- 15 Ounces of Frozen Corn
- 1 Tablespoon of Chili Powder

- ❖ 1 Tablespoon of Onion Powder
- ❖ 2 Tablespoons of Dried Parsley
- ❖ 16 Ounces of Mild Salsa
- ❖ 26 Ounces of peeled and diced tomatoes
- ❖ 27 Ounces of Chicken Broth
- ❖ Salt and Pepper
- ❖ 1 Teaspoon of Garlic Powder
- ❖ 2 Tablespoons of Olive Oil
- ❖ 1 Diced Onion
- ❖ 3 Cloves of minced garlic
- ❖ 32 Ounces of Black Beans

Instructions:

Turn Instant Pot to the 'sauté' function, then add olive oil, then add garlic and onions, and stir for 5 minutes, add the rest of the ingredients into the Instant Pot, except for the beans and the corn, close the lid.

Set timer for 8 minutes at high level pressure, when 8 minutes is up, press the quick release before open the lid, remove the chicken from the Instant Pot and transport it to a cutting boardand shred , then put back into the instant pot.

Mix the corn and the beans into the Instant Pot now, and stir around with a spoon , set to the 'simmer' mode and bring the food to a boil . Allow the food to cool down and then pour into individual bowls to serve.

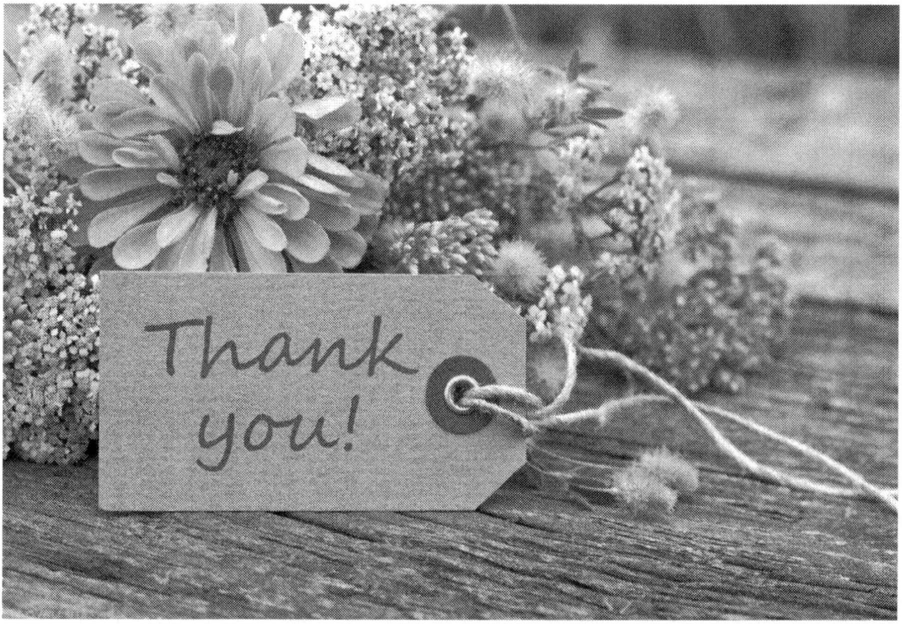
Thank
you!

Chapter 4: Pork Recipes

♣ Pork Ribs Spicy Dish

Ingredients:

- 2½ pound boneless pork ribs
- 1 cup chicken broth
- 12 teaspoon ground coriander
- 1 cup homemade tomato sauce
- ¼ teaspoon ground allspice
- Freshly ground black pepper
- 2 tablespoons balsamic vinegar
- 2 teaspoons mustard powder
- 2 minced garlic cloves,
- 1 teaspoon dried crushed thyme
- 1 teaspoon smoked paprika
- ½ teaspoon ground cumin
- 2 tablespoons olive oil
- 1 large sliced onion

Instructions: In a large bowl, mix together the garlic, thyme and spices. Add the pork ribs and coat with spice mixture generously. In another small bowl, mix together broth, tomato sauce, vinegar and mustard.

Pour the oil in the Instant Pot and select "Sauté." Add the onion and cook for about 5 minutes.

Select "Cancel" and place the pork over the ribs. Pour broth mixture over the ribs. Secure the lid and select "Meat" and just use the default time of 35 minutes. Select the "Cancel" button and carefully do a natural release. Remove the lid and serve and enjoy.

⚜ Mexican Pork Dish

Ingredients:

- 2 ½ pounds of pork shoulder
- ¾ cups of chicken broth
- ½ teaspoon of garlic powder
- ¼ teaspoon of dry seasoning
- ¼ teaspoon of dry oregano
- Black pepper salt
- 1 tablespoon of vegetable oil
- 1 ½ teaspoons of cumin
- 2 bay leaves
- 3 chipotle peppers in adobo sauce
- 5 cloves of minced garlic

Instructions: Mix the adobo seasoning with cumin garlic powder and oregano in a small bowl to make the rub.

Season the pork with some salt and pepper then rub it with the dry seasoning.

Heat the oil in an instant pot then brown in it the pork shoulder for 5 min.

Stir in the rest of the ingredients.

Cover the pot and bring it to pressure then cook it for 45 min on high pressure.

Once the time is up, release the pressure naturally.

Drain the pork shoulder and shred it then stir it back into the juices then serve and enjoy.

❖ Pork Taco Dish

Ingredients:

- ❖ Salt and lack pepper
- ❖ 3 ½ pound of pork shoulder roast
- ❖ 2 teaspoons of cumin
- ❖ 2 teaspoons of dry coriander
- ❖ 4 cups of beef broth
- ❖ 1 teaspoon of garlic powder
- ❖ ¼ teaspoon of paprika
- ❖ ½ yellow onion, cut into chunks
- ❖ 2 teaspoons of dry oregano

Instructions:

Stir all the ingredients in a pressure cooker then season them with some salt and pepper.

Put on the lid and cook them for 40 min.

Once time is up, use the natural method to release the pressure.

Drain the pork shoulder and shred it then stir back into the pot.

Fill the taco shells with the shredded roast then serve them and enjoy.

❖ Fruity Pork Dish

Ingredients:

- ❖ 1 1/2 pound boneless pork tenderloin
- ❖ Freshly ground black pepper
- ❖ 2 cups of cored and chopped apples
- ❖ ½ cup fresh apple juice
- ❖ Pinch of salt
- ❖ 2/3 cup fresh pitted cherries
- ❖ 1/3 cup chopped celery stalk
- ❖ 1/3 cup chopped onion

Instsructions:

Place all the ingredients in the Instant Pot and secure the lid. Select "Meat" and just use the default time of 40 minutes. Select the "Cancel" button and carefully do a quick release. Remove the lid , serve and enjoy.

⚜ Sauté Pork Steak Dish

Ingredients:

- ❖ Black pepper and Salt
- ❖ 5 pork steaks, diced
- ❖ 2 tablespoons of butter
- ❖ 2 tablespoons of cornstarch
- ❖ 27 ounces of canned beans sprouts
- ❖ 14 ounces of chicken broth
- ❖ ½ cup of water
- ❖ 1/3 cup of soy sauce
- ❖ 10 Sliced white mushroom
- ❖ 3 stalks of diced celery
- ❖ 1 finely chopped yellow onion
- ❖ 4 tablespoons of molasses
- ❖ 1 tablespoon of vegetable oil

Instructions: Whisk the cornstarch with water and set them aside.

Press the sauté button on the instant pot then heat the oil in it.

Add the mushroom with onion, steak dices and celery then sauté them for 7 min.

Stir in the remaining ingredients then season them with some salt and pepper.

Put on the lid and cook them for 15 min on high pressure.

Once the time is up, use the natural method to release the pressure.

Serve your pork steak sauté warm with some rice and enjoy.

⚜ Baby Pork Ribs Dish

Ingredients:

- 3 racks baby back ribs
- 1 cup of water
- 4 tablespoon granulated garlic powder
- 1 tablespoon coriander
- 2 cups smoky barbecue sauce
- 2 tablespoon onion powder
- 1 tablespoon cumin
- 1 small peeled and diced onion

Instructions:

In a bowl, evenly blend together the garlic powder, onion powder, cumin and coriander to create a seasoning blend.

Cut the ribs in half so that they can easily fit in the Power Cooker. Season them evenly

Place 1 cup of water in the Power Cooker. Add the Ribs side by side. Add the diced onion and evenly pour the BBQ sauce over the ribs.

Place the lid on the Power Cooker, lock the lid and switch the pressure release valve to closed.

Press the SOUP/STEW button and then press the COOK TIME SELECTOR button until the time is 35 Min.

Once the time is up, the cooker will automatically switch to KEEP WARM. Switch the pressure release valve to open. When the steam is completely released, remove the lid.

Serve and enjoy!

Boneless Pork Chops Dish

Ingredients:

- 4 boneless pork chops
- Salt & Black pepper
- 15 ounces of canned, drained artichoke hearts
- ½ cup of finely chopped sundried tomato
- 2 tablespoons of purpose flour
- 1 tablespoon of vegetable oil
- ½ cup of chicken stock
- ½ cup of white wine
- ¼ cup of drained capers
- 2 finely chopped shallots
- 1 clove of minced garlic

Instructions:

Press the sauté button on the instant pot then heat the oil in it.

Add the shallots with pork chops and brown them for 7 min.

Stir in the remaining ingredients then season them with some salt and pepper.

Put on the lid and cook it for 7 min on high pressure.

When the time is up, use the natural method to release the pressure.

Allow the pork chops to rest for 5 min then serve them and enjoy.

⚜ Pork Roast

Ingredients:

- ❖ A 1 pound shoulder pork
- ❖ 1 ½ cloves of crushed garlic
- ❖ 1 peeled cooking apple, cut quarters
- ❖ ½ tablespoon of olive oil
- ❖ 1/4 cup apple juice
- ❖ ½ tablespoon of finely chopped rosemary
- ❖ Seasoning to taste
- ❖ 1 ½ tablespoons of mustard

Instructions: Coat the meat with the mustard.

Coat the bottom of the cooker with the oil and set your stove to Medium-high.

Sear the outside of the meat, then put aside for 2 minutes then add whatever liquid you are using to the pot. and add the roast back in.

Add everything else and secure the lid. Cook for round about 45 minutes. Do check that the internal temperature of the meat is 160 degrees Fahrenheit

Take the meat out and set it aside

Blend together all the remaining juices, and serve with the roast.

⚜ Yummy Pork Curry With Coconut

Ingredients:

- ❖ 6 pounds pork shoulder , cut into pieces
- ❖ Salt and black pepper
- ❖ 4 pounds small red potatoes,cut into sixths
- ❖ 2 tablespoon vegetable oil
- ❖ 16 ounce can Thai green curry paste
- ❖ 60-ounce can coconut milk

Instructions: Heat the broiler and put the pork in, Salt and pepper seasoning. Put on a baking sheet and broil until well-browned on both sides.

Spread the potatoes pieces in a slow cooker. Sprinkle salt and pepper. Heat the oil in a pan, and then put curry paste. Fry about 6 minutes and mix coconut milk. Cook for another 6 minutes.

Remove the pork from oven, drain liquid and place the pork in your slow cooker along with potatoes. Put green curry and coconut milk-mixture over.

Cook on LOW for 6 to 8 hours. Shred the pork by using forks. Serve with the brown rice.

⁕ Honey Pork Chops Dish

Ingredients:

- 4 pounds Boneless Pork Chops
- 1 teaspoons Cinnamon
- 1 teaspoons Cloves, Ground
- Preparation
- 1 teaspoons Sea salt grounded
- 1/2 teaspoons Black Pepper
- 1/2 cups Honey
- 1 teaspoons peel and mince Ginger
- 4 tablespoons Mustard
- 1 tablespoons Maple Syrup

Instructions: Sprinkle the pork pieces along with salt and pepper. Place it in instant pot.

Sauté and brown the pork pieces on both sides.

Mix honey, cloves, maple syrup, dijon mustard, ginger, and cinnamon. Put over the pork chops, lock the lid. Cook for 20 minutes, then serve and enjoy.

♣ Cabbage Pork Chops Dish

Ingredients:

- ❖ 4 thick-cut Pork Chops
- ❖ 1 teaspoon fennel seeds
- ❖ 3/4 cup meat stock
- ❖ 2 teaspoons of flour
- ❖ 1 teaspoon salt
- ❖ 1 teaspoon pepper
- ❖ 1 small head cabbage
- ❖ 1 tablespoon vegetable oil

Instructions : Sprinkle with fennel, salt and pepper on the pork chops

Slicing the cabbage in half and then set aside.

Pre-heated pressure cooker, on medium-high heat without the lid, add oil, and brown all of the chops, then put aside

Add the cabbage slices into the empty pressure cooker.

On top of the cabbage arrange the pork chops ,overlapping as needed. Pour any juice from the chops and meat stock around the edges. Close and lock the lid

Cook for 8 minutes at high pressure.

When time is up, open the pressure cooker with the Normal release - release pressure

Transfer the cabbage and pork chops to a serving platte

Bring the left-over juices in the pressure cooker to a boil and whisk-in the flour.

Pour thickened sauce on top of cabbage and pork chop platter and serve.

✤ Pork Vindaloo

Ingredients:

- 2 piece fresh peeled ginger, about 3 inch
- 6 tablespoons canola oil
- 1 teaspoon fenugreek seeds
- 1 teaspoon turmeric
- 3 to 5 teaspoons ground Indian red chile
- 3 teaspoons salt
- 2 1-inch piece cassia
- 2 teaspoon sugar
- 4 tablespoons tamarind paste
- 2 tablespoon white vinegar
- 4 tablespoons coriander seeds
- 2 teaspoon cumin seeds
- 1 teaspoon brown mustard seeds
- 10 to 12 cloves
- 6 to 8 black cardamom pods
- 40 black peppercorns
- 6 medium yellow thinly sliced onions

- ❖ 8 pounds pork shoulder, cut into 1 1/2- to 2-inch cubes
- ❖ 20 minced garlic gloves
- ❖ 8 serrano minced chiles

Instructions: Preheat the slow cooker on high for 15 minutes. prepare 1 inch of the julienned ginger and set aside for garnish. Mince or the remaining ginger.

Warm the oil in a pan, then add fenugreek seeds. Put the lid on immediately.

When sputtering is stopped, then add onions. Sauté them until golden brown. Put onions into slow cooker along with pork, garlic, ginger, serrano chiles, red chile, salt and turmeric.

Cook for 3 1/2 hours on low. Grind the coriander seeds, sugar, mustard seeds, cardamom, cloves, peppercorns, cassia, and cumin seeds.

Mix these spices into pork and cook extra 30 minutes. Remove from heat and add tamarind pulp and vinegar. Garnish with julienned ginger and enjoy.

Chapter 5: Beef Recipes

✣ Mogolian Beef

Ingredients:

- •2 pounds steak, cut 1/4" strips
- •1/2 cup soy sauce
- •1/2 cup water
- •1 tablespoon vegetable oil
- •4 cloves minced garlic
- •2 tablespoon cornstarch
- •3 tablespoons water
- •2/3 cup dark brown sugar
- •1/2 teaspoon minced fresh ginger
- •3 green onions, sliced into 1-inch pieces

Instructions: Seasoning the beef with salt and pepper. Put oil in the cooking pot and select browning. When oil begins to sizzle, brown the meat then transfer meat to a plate

Add the garlic and saute 1 minute. Add soy sauce, 1/2 cup water, brown sugar, and ginger then stir evenly

Add browned beef and any accumulated juices. Select High Pressure. Set timer for 14 minutes.

When the time is up use a quick pressure release. and remove the lid

Combine the cornstarch and 3 tablespoons water, whisking until smooth. Add cornstarch mixture to the sauce in the pot stirring constantly. Select Simmer and bring to a boil, stirring constantly until sauce thickens. Stir in green onions, serve and enjoy.

🌶 Barbacoa Salsa Beef

Ingredients:

- Meat enough for 30 tacos
- 4 canned of chipotles in adobo sauce and minced
- 1/2 bunch of fresh chopped cilantro,
- 16 cups of either beef or chicken stock
- 5 bay leaves
- 1/2 medium roughly chopped onion,
- 1/2 head of minced garlic
- 1/2 tablespoon of Salt Kosher approved
- Juice extracted from 4 limes
- 1/2 teaspoon grounded cloves
- 1/2 cup of apple cider vinegar
- 8 pounds of beef brisket

- To serve:
- 30 corn tortillas, warmed
- Diced onions
- Minced cilantro
- Salsa

Instructions:

Put chipotle peppers along with sauce, garlic, clove, lime juice, red onion, cilantro, salt and vinegar in a slow cooker until mixed well.

Put brisket on the top of the mixture. Pour the stock over the meat, and then put bay leaves on the top. Mix the meat in the sauce.

Cover the slow cooker and cook for 9 to 10 hours on low. Place meat to a baking sheet and shred meat with forks. Shredded beef in a large bowl.

Pour cooking liquid over the top. Serve along with cilantro, onion, tortillas, and salsa.

⚜ Beef Dumplings Stew

Ingredients:

- ❖ 4 pounds of beef stew meat
- ❖ Salt and Black pepper
- ❖ 1 ½ can of biscuits diced dough,
- ❖ 1 can of cream of mushroom soup
- ❖ 8 ounces of sliced mushroom,
- ❖ 23 ounces of frozen mixed veggies
- ❖ 12 ounces of French onion soup
- ❖ 2 cups of water
- ❖ 1 tablespoon of Worcestershire sauce

Instructions: Stir the water with beef stew meat, mushroom soup and mushroom, water, Worcestershire sauce, onion soup, a pinch of salt and pepper in an instant pot then put on the lid and cook them for 30 min on high pressure.

When the time is up, use the natural method to release the pressure.

Stir in the veggies and press the sauté button then simmer them for 8 min.

Top the stew with the dough dices then put on the lid and cooks them for 5 min on high pressure.

When the time is up, use the natural method to release the pressure. Serve warm and enjoy.

Italian Beef Dish

Ingredients:

- 8 pounds of Beef Roast
- 32 ounces of Whole canned Tomatoes
- 1/2 teaspoons of Black Pepper
- 4 whole Bay Leaves
- 1 teaspoons of mince Garlic,
- 6 medium Garlic, pieces
- 2 tablespoon of Wine Vinegar
- 1/2 cups of Water
- 4 teaspoons of Bouillon, Beef, Granules
- 1 teaspoons of Pickling Spice
- 2 teaspoon of Salt

Instructions: Cut the maximum fat from meat and place in instant pot. Mix all of the ingredients over beef.

Lock the lid on pot and cook for 40 minutes. Remove the bay leaves just before you serve.

♣ Corned Beef Dish

Ingredients:

- 2.5 pound Corned Beef
- 2 cups of Chicken stock
- 1 clove of garlic smashed
- 1 pound of red potatoes
- 2 cups of water
- 4 allspice Whole
- 2 sprigs of Fresh thyme
- 2 bay leaves
- 2 tablespoon whole black pepper corns
- 1 onion white diced
- 4 carrots peeled and cut into 3 inch pieces
- 1/2 head of green cabbage cut into 4 pieces

Instructions: Place the corned beef, stock, water bay leaves, peppercorns, allspice, thyme, onion and garlic.

Place the lid on the Power Cooker, lock the lid

Press the Chicken/Meat button, 3x to 60 min.

When the time is up, the cooker will automatically switch to KEEP WARM. Switch the pressure release valve to open. When the steam is completely released, remove the lid. Press the CANCEL Button.

Remove the corn beef from the broth. Add in the potatoes, carrots, and cabbage.

Place the lid on the Power Cooker, lock the lid and switch the pressure release valve to closed. Press the Fish/Vegetable, 3x set to 10 minutes.

When time is up, and the steam is completely released, remove the lid. Serve and enjoy!

⚜ Curry Beef Dish

Ingredients:

- ❖ 18 ounces diced beef
- ❖ 2 cloves chopped garlic
- ❖ 1 can of coconut milk
- ❖ 1 jar of pasta tomato sauce
- ❖ 3 large diced potatoes
- ❖ 2 ½ tablespoon mild curry powder
- ❖ 1 tablespoon grainy wine mustard
- ❖ 2 large chopped onions
- ❖ Large glug of olive Oil

Instructions: Heat pressure cooker add oil with the lid of

Add onions & garlic and caramelise

Add mustard, potatoes and cook for a further 2 minute

Add diced beef and brown

Add curry powder and cook for 3 minutes

Pour in tomato sauce and coconut milk

Put lid on the pressure cooker and cook for 10 minutes

Serve and enjoy!

❖ Beef Rice Noodle Soup

Ingredients:

- ❖ 7 Cups of Chicken Broth
- ❖ 1 ½ Pounds of boneless Beef Sirloin
- ❖ 1 Tablespoon of sambal oelek
- ❖ ¼ Cup of Mirin
- ❖ 1 Sliced Yellow Onion
- ❖ 2 Tablespoons of Rice Vinegar
- ❖ 4 Ounces of dried Rice Stick Noodles
- ❖ ½ Cup of Soy Sauce
- ❖ 8 Dried stemmed Mushrooms of Your Choice
- ❖ 1 Tablespoon of fresh Minced Ginger

Instructions: In the Instant Pot, put the beef, chicken broth, onion, soy sauce, ginger, mushrooms of your choice, vinegar, and sambal oelek

Stir all of the ingredients together with a spoon, then close the lid

Set the Instant Pot to a high pressure option and the timer to 15 minutes

When time is up, press the quick release valve to release the pressure in the Instant Pot

Mix the rice noodles and the Mirin into the Instant Pot

Stir everything in the Instant Pot with a spoon for 3 minutes

Set the timer on the Instant Pot to 2 minutes and the pressure level to high

At the end of the 2 minutes, press the quick release valve again to release the pressure

Carefully remove the lid from the Instant Pot

Stir the soup for 2 minutes. Serve and enjoy.

⁕ Chilli Beef Dish

Ingredients:

- ❖ 2.5 pounds lean beef
- ❖ 4 cups crushed tomatoes
- ❖ 1 teaspoon cumin
- ❖ 1 teaspoon ground coriander
- ❖ 1/2 cup beef stock

- ❖ 1 large diced onion
- ❖ 1 tablespoon crushed red pepper flakes
- ❖ 1 tablespoon sugar
- ❖ 2 tablespoon grape seed oil
- ❖ 1/3 cup dried red beans ,soak beans overnight
- ❖ 1/3 cup dried black beans ,soak beans overnight
- ❖ 1/3 cup dried navy beans, soak beans overnight
- ❖ 1/4 cup chili powder
- ❖ 1 tablespoon sea salt
- ❖ Sour cream for garnish
- ❖ Cheddar cheese for garnish

Instructions: Place the inner pot in the Power Cooker. Place the oil in the inner pot. Press Chicken/Meat button. Add the beef and onions. Cook for 6 minutes. Add the spices and cook for 2 minute,then add the remaining ingredients.

Lock the lid and switch the pressure release valve to closed.

Press the Warm/Cancel button.

Press the Soup/Stew button and then press the Time Adjustment button until about 20 minutes

When the time is up, the cooker will automatically switch to Keep Warm. Switch the pressure release valve to open. remove the lid. When the steam is completely release. To serve,Garnish with sour cream and shredded cheddar cheese and enjoy.

BBQ Beef

Ingredients:

- 1 1/3 Cup of frozen Beef Roast
- 2 Teaspoons of Honey
- ¼ Teaspoon of BBQ Seasoning
- 1 Cup of Water
- ½ Cup oflow sugar Ketchup

Instructions: Spray your Instant Pot with a nonstick spray first

Place the roast beef and water into the pot

Press the 'meat' button on the Instant Pot and place the lid on

Set the Instant Pot for 8 minutes

Mix the honey, ketchup, BBQ seasoning, and water in a bowl

When the time is up, press the quick release valve on the Instant Pot to release the pressure

Remove the lid from the Instant Pot and transfer all of the beef inside to a cutting board

Trim off any fat or skin on the beef as desired, and then shred it apart into mid to small sized chunks

Discard the beef broth that's in the Instant Pot, and then place the pulled beef back into the pot

Pour the BBQ sauce over the meat inside

Select the Sauté option on the Instant Pot

Cook the meat and BBQ sauce at the sauté option for 3 minutes

Serve with hamburger buns, beans, or French fries.

♣ Burger Beef With Mushroom

Ingredients:

- ❖ 1/2 pound of ground, lean sirloin
- ❖ 1/3 tablespoon of pre-mixed Italian herb seasoning
- ❖ 4 ounces of cream of mushroom soup
- ❖ 3 ounces of cleaned and sliced mushrooms
- ❖ 2 tablespoons of skimmed milk

Instructions: Season the meat and shape into two patties.

Set your stove to Medium-high. Sear the burgers by frying for round about three minutes, remember to flip.

Add the soup and mushrooms. Top off with the milk.

Secure the lid and heat until a low pressure is achieved. Cook for about 10 minutes.

Then take the lid off. Set the meat aside in a warmer drawer.

Remove the excess fat from the liquid, and simmer the sauce until it has thickened before serving.

♣ Onion Beef Soup

Ingredients:

- ❖ 7 Cups of Beef Broth
- ❖ 3 Tablespoons of Cognac
- ❖ 2 Meaty Beef Ribs

- ❖ Salt and Pepper
- ❖ 2 Pounds of sliced Onion
- ❖ ¼ Teaspoon of All Spice
- ❖ 1 Tablespoon of Potato Starch
- ❖ 2 Tablespoons of unsalted Butter
- ❖ 1 Tablespoon of Olive Oil

Instructions: Melt the butter and olive oil in the Instant Pot to the browning setting

Add onion into the Instant Pot and stir it until brown

Add cognac into the mix to make a juice

Transfer the onions that are now soaked in the juice over to a bowl

In the Instant Pot, add the allspice, broth, salt and pepper, wine, and beef

Close the lid and time it for 45 minutes on high pressure

When the time is up, press the quick release valve to release the pressure

Remove the lid from the Instant Pot and then transfer the ribs over to a cutting board

Chop up the meat and get rid of all of the bones

Place the meat into the Instant Pot and mix it with the onions and juices

Shut the lid and time the ingredients to cook for 5 minutes at a high pressure

Press the browning button on the Instant Pot and bring the food inside to a simmer

Combine one tablespoon of water and potato starch in a bowl and whisk them neatly together

Pour the potato starch into the Instant Pot, and stir it in with the rest of the ingredients while cooking for one to two minutes

Close off the pressure cooker serve and enjoy.

Chapter 6: Turkey Recipes

❖ Celery Turkey Noodle Soup

Ingredients:

- 6 Cups of Turkey Stock
- 4 peeled and cut Carrots
- 1 Rib of Diced Celery
- 1 Tablespoon of Butter
- 1 Diced Onion
- 2 Cups of Diced Turkey Meat
- Salt and Pepper
- Egg Noodles (prepared as on instructions packaging)

Instructions: Set the Instant Pot to the sauté function

Place the butter into your Instant Pot, when melted, place the onions in

Add carrots and celery and sauté them in the melted butter as well for 5 minutes

Add the turkey meat and turkey stock into the Instant Pot next and close the lid

Set the timer on the Instant Pot for 5 minutes at a high pressure

When time is up, shut off the press cooker with the quick release method

Remove the lid and season the turkey soup inside with as much salt and pepper as desired

While the turkey soup is cooling down, place your cooked noodles into individual eating bowls

Pour the turkey soup over the noodles, and enjoy.

♣ Braised Turkey Dish

Ingredients:

- 7 pounds skin-on, bone-in turkey breast
- 1 tablespoon fresh minced thyme,
- 1 tablespoon fresh minced rosemary,
- Freshly ground black pepper
- 1 chopped celery stalk,
- 1 large chopped onion
- 3 tablespoons cornstarch
- 3 tablespoons water
- 14 ounce chicken broth

Instructions:

Arrange a steamer trivet in the Instant Pot. Place the celery, onion, herbs and broth in the Instant Pot. put turkey breast on top and sprinkle with black pepper.

Secure the lid and cook under "Manual" and "High Pressure" for about 10 minutes. Select the "Cancel" button and carefully do a quick release.

Remove the lid and transfer the turkey breast into a bowl.skim off the fat from the surface of the broth and then strain it.

In a small bowl, dissolve the cornstarch in water.

Return the broth to the Instant Pot and select "Sauté" slowly. Add the cornstarch mixture, stirring continuously. Cook for about 5 minutes. Select the "Cancel" and transfer the gravy into a serving bowl.

Cut the turkey breast into desired sized slices and serve alongside the gravy.

❖ Turkey Stock with Carrots

Ingredients:

- ❖ 1 large white onion
- ❖ 5 bay leaves
- ❖ 4 carrots
- ❖ 4 celery sticks
- ❖ Turkey carcass pieces
- ❖ 1 teaspoon black peppercorns
- ❖ Water

Instructions: Fill half of a slow cooker with turkey carcass

Add all other Ingredients, and fill with water.

Leave about an inch of room on top.

Cook on low heat for about 6-8 hours.

Pull out the carcass pieces and veggies and discard.

Place strainer over a bowl.

Pour stock from the cooker. Serve and enjoy!

⁕ Honey Turkey Breast

Ingredients:

- ❖ 2 turkey breast
- ❖ 2 cup frank's red hot
- ❖ 1/2 cup honey
- ❖ 1/2 tsp Black pepper
- ❖ 8 tsp melted butter

Instructions:

Place turkey breast into a slow cooker pot.

Add frank's red hot, honey, pepper and melted butter In a small bowl. Stir until smooth.

Pour half of the sauce over turkey breast. Put the remaining sauce in fridge.

Cover cooker and start heating on low mode heat for about 4-5 hours.

Heat remaining sauce in the cooker in microwave until warmed.

Remove turkey breast from the cooker, remove skin and bone. Slice and serve.

⁕ Turkey Soup

Ingredients:

- ❖ 6 turkey necks
- ❖ ½ teaspoon of dry oregano

- ❖ Black pepper and Salt
- ❖ 3 cups of water
- ❖ 1 cup of rice
- ❖ 2 diced carrots,
- ❖ 1 tablespoon of butter
- ❖ ½ teaspoon of dry rosemary
- ❖ 2 stalks of diced celery,
- ❖ 1 small finely chopped onion

Instructions: Press the sauté button on the instant pot then melt the butter

Add the onion with carrot and celery then cook them for 5 minutes

Stir in the remaining ingredients then season them with some salt and pepper.

Put on the lid and cook it for 15 min on high pressure.

When the time is up, use the natural method to release the pressure.

Adjust the seasoning of the soup then serve it warm and enjoy.

⚜ BBQ Sauce Turkey with Oatmeal

Ingredients:

- ❖ 2 cup oatmeal
- ❖ 2 lb Ground turkey

- ❖ 2 can tomato sauce
- ❖ 1/4 tsp of Pepper
- ❖ BBQ sauce
- ❖ 1 cup diced onion
- ❖ 2 tsp of Salt

Instructions: Combine turkey, tomato sauce, oatmeal, onion, salt and pepper in a bowl, mix well

Place in a bread loaf pan. Place the pan inside of a slow cooker.

Cover the cooker and Set to high power cooking heat for about 3-4 hours.

Brush the top of meatloaf with BBQ sauce, then place in oven, Broil for 3 minutes, then serve and enjoy.

⚜ Turkey Breast Soup With Cornstarch

Ingredients:

- ❖ 2 envelope onion soup mix
- ❖ 6 tbsp Butter
- ❖ 2 honeysuckle turkey breast
- ❖ 4 tbsp of Water
- ❖ Salt and pepper
- ❖ 4 tbsp of Cornstarch

Instructions: Rinse turkey breast and pat dry. Marinates Onions soup mis all over

Place butter in bottom of a slow cooker.

Place turkey breast in cooker with breast side down.

Cover cooker and start heating on low mode heat for about 7 hours.

Use foil to tent turkey. Pour juices in the bottom of the cooker.

Mix cornstarch and water until smooth together in a bowl.

Add cornstarch mixture into the saucepan with drippings.

Whisk over medium heat. Add salt and pepper.Slice and serve with gravy.

⚜ Turkey Breast Roll

Ingredients:

- ❖ 3 pound boneless & skinless turkey breast. Evenly sliced
- ❖ 2 tablespoons unsalted butter
- ❖ 3 celery stalks, roughly Chopped
- ❖ 500 ml Vegetable stock
- ❖ 12-ounce frozen cranberries
- ❖ 1 cup brown organic sugar
- ❖ 1 strip orange zest
- ❖ 3 small finely chopped red onions
- ❖ 1 cup whole milk

- 2 Tablespoons chopped parsley
- 2 Tablespoon olive oil
- 2 Tablespoons grainy mustard
- 3 crushed Garlic cloves,
- 2 Tablespoons twigs sage
- 1½ teaspoons salt, divided
- 1 pinch pepper
- 200 grams Dried breadcrumbs

Instructions: Turkey Roll

Pre heat the pressure cooker and add butter, garlic, sage, and celery using the saute setting until they are soft.

In a mixing bowl, add the bread crumbs, parsley, and 1 tablespoon salt. Mix thoroughly and then add milk.

After the vegetables have softened, add them to the mixing bowl containing the bread crumbs.

Lay out the sliced breasts and sprinkle with salt and pepper.

Gently place the bread mixture in the middle of the pieces leaving an allowance at the edges. Begin to roll tightly and tie together. Make sure the bread crumb mixture is securely tucked inside.

Add olive oil into the pressure cooker and adjust to high heat. Brown the rolls on all sides.

Place 2 spoons of grain mustard on the roast. Add the broth carefully not to mess the grain mustard.

Cook for 30 minutes at high pressure. When time is up, allow natural release method. Serve with cranberry sauce.

Cranberry sauce

Pour 12-ounce bag of fresh cranberries into a frying pan and transfer 1/2 cup into a mixing bowl.

Add 1 cup of sugar, 2 tablespoons water, and orange zest onto the pan and stir until the sugar dissolves.

Adjust your cooker settings to medium and cook for 10 minutes until the berries burst. Reduce the heat; add pepper, salt and pepper.

Let it rest for a while and serve.

Chapter 7: Lamb Recipes

♣ Mexican BBQ Lamb

Ingredients:

- 3 Kgs lamb shoulder
- 1 Spanish onion
- Toasted garlic bread
- 1 Small lime fruit
- Salt
- 3 Minced Garlic cloves,
- 19 oz can of Old El Paso Enchilada sauce
- 2 Tablespoons Olive oil

Instructions:

Marinate lamb for 24 hours in Old El Paso Enchilada sauce.

Add oil into the pressure cooker and set to sauté. Heat up for 2 minute. Add the onions, cook until soft.

On high pressure.Cook for 45 minutes

Heat the beans in and squeeze lime inside.

Shred the beef with a fork and serve with the beans and the toasted garlic bread.

⚜ Lamb Curry With Vegies

Ingredients:

- 1 pound ground lamb
- 2 tablespoons coconut oil
- 1 chopped onion,
- 1 teaspoon minced fresh ginger,
- 2 potatoes, peeled and chopped
- 1 cup fresh peas, shelled
- 1½ cups homemade tomato sauce
- 3 minced garlic cloves,
- 1 seeded and chopped Serrano pepper,
- 4 fresh finely chopped tomatoes
- 3 carrots, peeled and chopped
- 1 teaspoon ground coriander
- 1 teaspoon ground cumin
- 1 teaspoon red chili powder
- ¼ teaspoon ground turmeric
- ½ cup unsweetened coconut milk
- ¼ cup fresh cilantro, chopped

Instructions : Place the coconut oil in the Instant Pot and select "Sauté." Add the onion and garlic and cook for about 4 minutes.

Add ginger, garlic, Serrano pepper and spices and cook for about 1 minute. Add lamb and cook for about 5 minutes.

Select "Cancel" and stir in the remaining ingredients, except the cilantro. Next, secure the lid and select "Chili," using the default time of 30 minutes. Select the "Cancel" button and carefully do a natural release.

Remove the lid and stir in cilantro. Serve hot.

Lamb Soup

Ingredients:

- 1 Pound of Lamb Leg Meat
- 1 Teaspoon of Ground Coriander
- 2 Tablespoons of Minced Dill Fronds
- ½ Cup of Heavy Cream
- ½ Teaspoon of Salt
- 1 Cup of Fresh Peeled Onions
- 28 Ounces of Diced Tomatoes
- 2 Cups of Chicken Broth
- ½ Teaspoon of Ground Cinnamon
- 2 Tablespoons of Olive Oil

Instructions: Mix the lamb, coriander, cinnamon, and salt together in a bowl

Heat your pressure cooker to the browning mode

Pour the olive oil into the pressure cooker

Add onions into the pressure cooker and stir fry them for four minutes in the olive oil

Transfer the coated meat over to the cooker with the spices

Stir the meat in the sautéed onions for one to two minutes

Add broth, dill, and tomatoes into the Instant Pot and mix them all thoroughly together

Close a lid over the Instant Pot

Set the Instant Pot to a time of 15 minutes at a high pressure option

At the end of the 15 minutes, perform a quick release of the pressure inside

Remove the lid and stir in the cream with the lamb meat and other ingredients inside

Pour the soup into individual bowls and serve

⚜ Lamb Stew

Ingredients:

- ❖ 4 pounds of lamb stew meat
- ❖ 1 pound of baby potato, cut quartered
- ❖ 1 cup of ginger beer
- ❖ 2 tablespoons of vegetable oil
- ❖ 2 cloves of minced garlic,
- ❖ Black pepper and Salt

- ❖ 2 cups of beef stock
- ❖ ½ cup of dry prunes, soaked in warm water for 30 min
- ❖ ¼ cup of purpose flour
- ❖ 2 yellow sliced onions,
- ❖ 2 diced carrots

Instructions: Season the lamb with some salt and pepper then toss it in a large bowl with the purpose flour.

Press the sauté button on the instant pot then heat the oil in it.

Add the lamb meat and brown it for 7 min.

Stir in the remaining ingredients then season them with some salt and pepper.

Put on the lid and cook it for 25 min on high pressure.

Once the time is up, use the natural method to release the pressure. Serve and enjoy.

⚜ Lamb Shanks With Wine

Ingredients:

- ❖ 2 pounds of lamb shanks
- ❖ ½ cup of port wine
- ❖ 1 tablespoon of tomato paste
- ❖ 4 cloves of peeled garlic,
- ❖ 1 tablespoon of unsalted butter,
- ❖ 1 teaspoon of balsamic vinegar

- ❖ ½ teaspoon of dry rosemary
- ❖ Black pepper and Salt
- ❖ ½ cup of chicken stock
- ❖ 1 tablespoons of olive oil

Instructions:

Stir all the ingredients in an instant pot then season them with some salt and pepper.

Put on the lid and cook them for 30 min on high pressure.

Once the time is up, use the natural method to release the pressure.

Drain the lamb shanks then serve them and enjoy.

⚜ Lamb Roast

- ❖ Ingredients:
- ❖ 3 1/2 lb Lamb Chuck or Rump Roast
- ❖ 2 tablespoon vegetable oil
- ❖ 1 large onion, roughly chopped
- ❖ 1 1/2 cup water or Lamb broth
- ❖ 3 bay leaves

Instructions: Pat roast dry and season liberally with Lemon Pepper

Put oil in the cooking pot and select browning or Saute on the Instant Pot. When the oil begins to sizzle, brown meat on both sides. Remove roast from the cooking pot and add onions, water and bay leaves. Put roast back in the cooking pot on top of the onions.

Select High Pressure. Set timer for 75 minutes. When beep sounds turn off pressure cooker and use a natural pressure release to release pressure. carefully remove the lid.

Remove roast to a serving platter. Strain juices and discard onion and bay leaves. Thicken juices in cooking pot on simmer with a slurry of water and flour or cornstarch to make gravy.

Conclusion

Thank you again for downloading this book! I hope you have enjoyed reading and practicing making them. Eat healthy and staying happy is the key to longevity and health

If you've enjoyed this book, I would like to ask you kindly to leave me a positive review on Amazon, that will be much appreciated.

Warm Regards,
Elise Sanders

Printed in Poland
by Amazon Fulfillment
Poland Sp. z o.o., Wrocław